Contents

Dig it!

Dig! Dig! Earthworms make holes in soil. The holes make good homes.

Little
Pebble™

Little Creatures

Earthworms

3 8002 02357 364 7

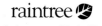
raintree
a Capstone company — publishers for children

Raintree is an imprint of Capstone Global Library Limited, a company incorporated in England and Wales having its registered office at 264 Banbury Road, Oxford, OX2 7DY – Registered company number: 6695582

www.raintree.co.uk
myorders@raintree.co.uk

Editorial Credits
Carrie Braulick Sheely, editor; Juliette Peters, designer; Wanda Winch, media researcher;
Tori Abraham, production specialist

ISBN 978-1-4747-2506-4 (hardcover)
20 19 18 17 16
10 9 8 7 6 5 4 3 2 1
ISBN 978-1-4747-2510-1 (paperback)
21 20 19 18 17
10 9 8 7 6 5 4 3 2 1

British Library Cataloguing in Publication Data
A full catalogue record for this book is available from the British Library.

Acknowledgements
We would like to thank the following for permission to reproduce photographs:
© Dwight Kuhn, 5, 10, 15, 19, 21; Alamy: Nature Photographers, Ltd, 17; Minden Pictures: Ch'ien Lee, 13; Newscom: H/blickwinkel/picture alliance/H. Schmidbauer, 9; Shutterstock: blackeagleEMJ, 1, clearviewstock, 11, kzww, back cover (worm), 3 (all), 22, Number1411, soil image used as background throughout book, Picsfive, note design, schankz, 7, wawritto, cover

Every effort has been made to contact copyright holders of material reproduced in this book. Any omissions will be rectified in subsequent printings if notice is given to the publisher.

All the Internet addresses (URLs) given in this book were valid at the time of going to press. However, due to the dynamic nature of the Internet, some addresses may have changed, or sites may have changed or ceased to exist since publication. While the author and publisher regret any inconvenience this may cause readers, no responsibility for any such changes can be accepted by either the author or the publisher.

Printed in China.

Worms like wet soil.

Hot sun dries their skin.

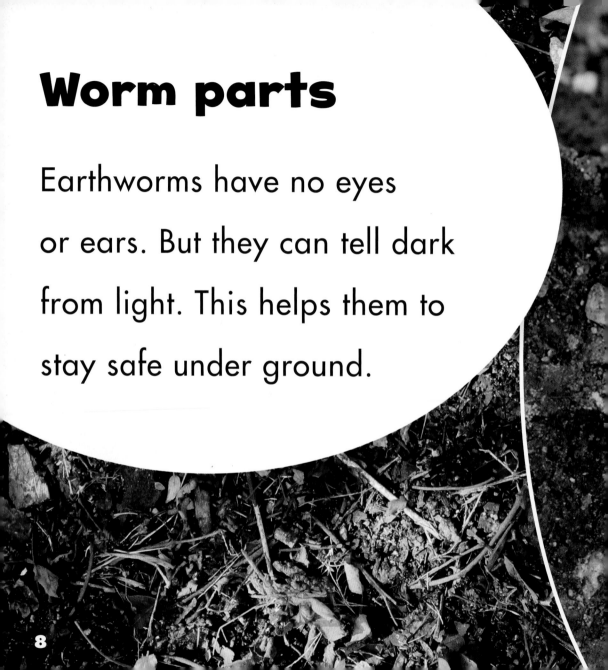

Worm parts

Earthworms have no eyes or ears. But they can tell dark from light. This helps them to stay safe under ground.

Wiggle! Tiny hairs help worms to move. They grip the soil.

hair

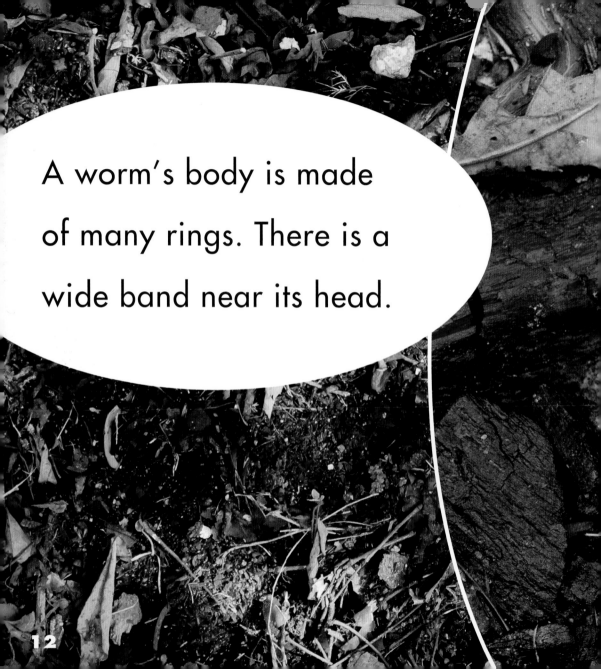

A worm's body is made of many rings. There is a wide band near its head.

Lunchtime

Munch! Earthworms eat
dead plants.
They eat tiny rocks too.
The rocks grind the food.

Worms eat and eat.

Their waste helps plants

to grow.

worm

Baby worms

Earthworms lay eggs.

The eggs are inside a cocoon.

19

Baby worms hatch out.

They eat, dig and grow.

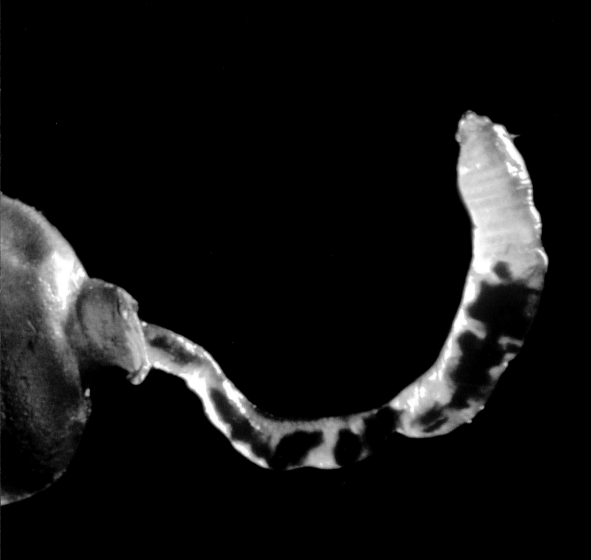

21

Glossary

band thick ring

cocoon covering made of slime; worms make a cocoon to hold their eggs until they are ready to hatch

grind crush or wear down

hatch come out of an egg

Read more

Minibeast Babies (Animal Babies), Catherine Veitch (Raintree, 2014)

RSPB: First Book of Minibeasts, Anita Ganeri and David Chandler (A & C Black Publishers, 2011)

Worms (Creepy Crawlies), Sian Smith (Raintree, 2013)

Websites

www.bbc.co.uk/gardening/gardening_with_children/ didyouknow_worms.shtml
Find out some more fascinating facts about earthworms!

www.woodlandtrust.org.uk/naturedetectives/ activities/2015/06/minibeast-mansion/
Design and build your own minibeast mansion!

Comprehension questions

1. How do worms help plants to grow?
2. How do rocks help worms to eat?

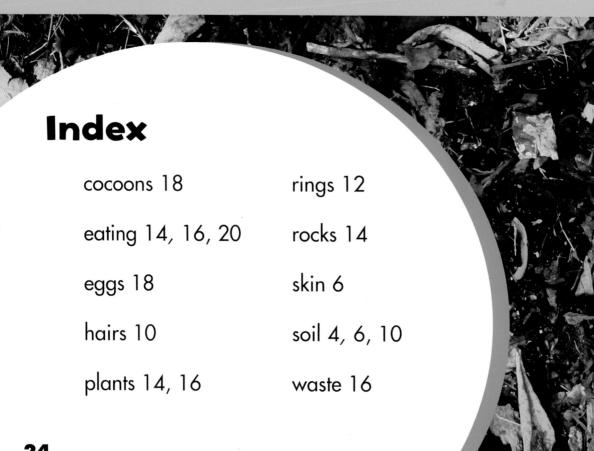

Index